Magnetic Forces

Elizabeth Lachner

The Rosen Publishing Group's
PowerKids Press™
New York

Published in 2009 by The Rosen Publishing Group, Inc.
29 East 21st Street, New York, NY 10010

Copyright © 2009 by The Rosen Publishing Group, Inc.

Book Design: Michael J. Flynn

Photo Credits: Cover, p. 13 (magnet) © Awe Inspiring Images/Shutterstock; pp. 3–8 (background),
10–32 (background) © clearviewstock; p. 5 (belt) © Alexander Kalina/Shutterstock; p. 5 (stud finder) ©
glinn/Shutterstock; p. 5 (refrigerator magnets) © Fotocrisis/Shutterstock; p. 5 (Tic-Tac-Toe) © Pling/Shutterstock;
p. 5 (phone) © stavklem/Shutterstock; p. 6 (magnetic field) http://upload.wikimedia.org/wikipedia/commons/
5/57/Magnet0873.png; p. 9 © Nikita Rogul/Shutterstock; p. 10 (magnet) © Morgan Lane Photography/
Shutterstock; p. 10 (paper clip) © Robyn Mackenzie/Shutterstock; p. 11 (lodestone) © Jens Mayer/
Shutterstock; p. 12 (steel rod) © Bjorn Heller/Shutterstock; p. 12 (round magnets) © Diana Rich/
Shutterstock; p. 12 (globe) © argus/Shutterstock; p. 15 (Faraday) © Hulton Archive/Getty Images; p. 16
(electromagnet) © Stockbyte/Getty Images; p. 19 (Earth) © Andrea Danti/Shutterstock; p. 21 (magnetosphere)
http://upload.wikimedia.org/wikipedia/commons/f/f3/Magnetosphere_rendition.jpg; p. 22 © Walter S. Becker/
Shutterstock; p. 24 (compass) © Tischenko Irina/Shutterstock; p. 26 (train) © Koichi/Getty Images;
p. 27 (MRI) © Bernhard Lelle/Shutterstock; p. 28 (MRI machine) http://upload.wikimedia.org/wikipedia/
commons/b/bd/Modern_3T_MRI.JPG; p. 29 (pipe deck on oil rig) © Ingvar Tjostheim/Shutterstock;
p. 30 (magnet) © Cico/Shutterstock.

Library of Congress Cataloging-in-Publication Data

Lachner, Elizabeth.
  Magnetic forces / Elizabeth Lachner.
      p. cm. -- (Real life readers)
  Includes index.
  ISBN: 978-1-4358-0155-4
  6-pack ISBN: 978-1-4358-0156-1
  ISBN 978-1-4358-2986-2 (library binding)
  1. Magnetism—Juvenile literature. 2. Electromagnetism—Juvenile literature. I. Title.
  QC753.7.L325 2009
  538--dc22
                                      2008042330

Manufactured in the United States of America

Contents

Magnets Around Us

Have you ever seen or used a magnet? What were you able to do with it? Are you curious about how magnets work?

In this book, we'll look at magnets and their forces. We'll see why some things are **attracted** to or **repelled** by magnets while others aren't affected at all. We'll read about natural and man-made magnets. We'll even look at Earth as a magnet!

Magnets come in many shapes and sizes. All magnets have **electric charges** that create an area around them that pulls some things toward them and pushes others away.

You may have performed experiments with magnets in science class. You may have used magnets to hold up pictures on your refrigerator or played a game that uses magnets. You've probably used magnets without even knowing it. Did you know computers, telephones, and TVs need magnets to work? Magnets are all around us!

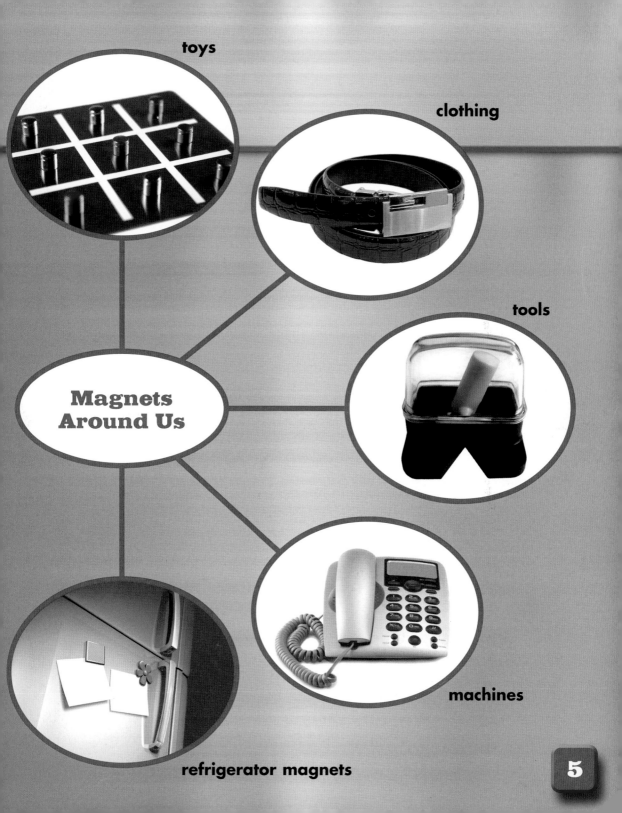

toys

clothing

tools

Magnets Around Us

machines

refrigerator magnets

5

Opposites Attract

If you've worked with magnets, you may have noticed that a magnet is attracted to one end or side of another magnet but is repelled by the opposite end or side. Every magnet has two **magnetic poles**—a north pole and a south pole. Each pole attracts the opposite pole of other magnets. For example, the north pole of one magnet attracts the south pole of another. The poles may be on opposite ends or opposite sides, depending on a magnet's shape.

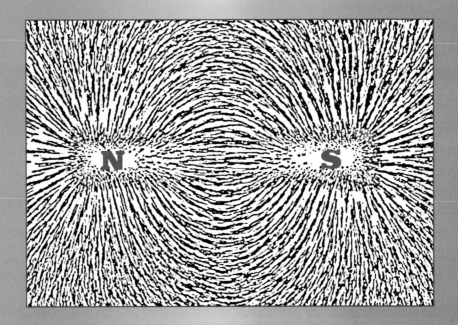

In this picture, iron filings, or tiny bits of iron, show the magnetic field around a bar magnet. This magnetic field is what affects objects surrounding the magnet.

Inside a Magnet

Like all matter, magnets are made of atoms. Each atom has a nucleus, or center, with a positive charge. Spinning around the nucleus are **particles** called electrons, which have a negative charge. Usually an atom's electrons are paired and spin in opposite directions, so that their magnetic fields balance out and there is no overall magnetic field. Sometimes, though, an atom has unpaired electrons that spin in the same direction. When lots of atoms with unpaired electrons line up in the same direction, they form areas called magnetic domains, which are like tiny magnets inside the **material**. When most of the domains line up with their north and south poles pointing in the same direction, the material becomes a magnet.

DEFINITION:	CHARACTERISTICS:
The area surrounding a magnet that results from spinning electrons.	• north and south poles • like poles repel; opposite poles attract • ability to attract and repel other magnetic objects

MAGNETIC FIELD

OBJECTS THAT HAVE A MAGNETIC FIELD:	OBJECTS THAT DON'T HAVE A MAGNETIC FIELD:
• credit cards • doorbells • alarm systems • computers	• books • plants • wooden furniture • plastic and glass containers

Magnetism

We know magnetism is a property of some materials that attract or repel other materials. Did you know that magnetism can be **permanent** or **temporary**?

Permanent Magnets

A permanent magnet is a material that keeps its magnetic properties once it has been magnetized. In materials that act as permanent magnets, their magnetic domains are permanently lined up. Today, most permanent magnets are made from alloys. Alloys are mixtures of metals. Almost all permanent magnets have iron, nickel, or cobalt. These metals are generally mixed with other elements to create magnets. For example, magnets made from nickel and cobalt are widely used in manufacturing.

Temporary Magnets

Besides attracting each other, magnets also attract other objects made of iron and nickel that aren't magnets. These objects can become magnetized

This clip has a permanent magnet. The magnet is attracted to the door of the refrigerator and keeps the clip in place.

through contact with a magnet. This contact causes the tiny magnetic domains in the object to line up. For example, if you rub a metal paper clip with a magnet, you can then use that paper clip to pick up a few more paper clips. The paper clip has become a temporary magnet. However, like all temporary magnets, it loses most of its magnetism when the magnetic field is removed. The weak magnetism that remains won't last very long. If you put the temporarily magnetized paper clip aside and then try to use it as a magnet later, it won't work.

The paper clips are attracted by their temporary magnetic fields.

Lodestones

The first magnets people discovered were naturally occurring permanent magnets called lodestones. Ancient Greeks and Chinese were astonished by the effects of lodestones thousands of years ago. Lodestones are a form of magnetite, which is a compound or mixture of the elements iron and oxygen. You can see magnetite in this quartz crystal.

Magnetic Fields

An astonishing fact about magnets is their ability to attract and repel one another even when they're not actually touching! How do they do it? Their magnetic fields make it possible. You can't see a magnetic field, but you can see its effects. Have you ever seen objects that seem to float above or between other objects? Perhaps you've seen a toy that has ring-shaped magnets with a stick through them in which the upper magnets seem to float above the lower ones. Maybe you've seen a globe that looks like it's hanging in midair. The forces produced by opposing magnetic fields keep the rings apart and the globe positioned in the air.

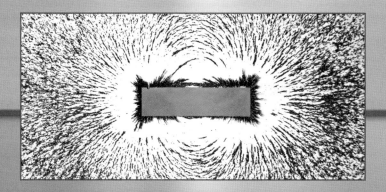

You can get an idea of the shape of a magnetic field by placing a bar magnet under a sheet of white paper and sprinkling iron filings over the paper. The way the filings line up shows the pattern of the magnetic field.

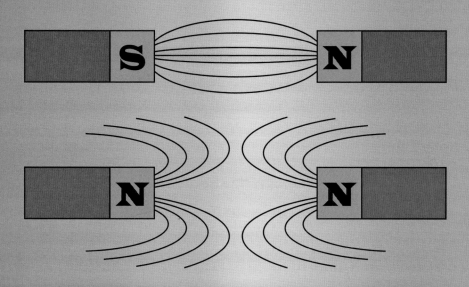

You can see how magnetic fields attract and repel by using two bar magnets. Place them under a sheet of white paper. First, position them so their north and south poles face each other and sprinkle iron filings on the paper. Next, position them so like poles face each other and sprinkle iron filings on the paper. What happens?

Electromagnetism

Magnetism and electricity are closely related. Electricity is the movement of electrons. Magnetism is produced by the movement of electrons. Magnetism and electricity both deal with electric current, which is the flow of electrons from a negatively charged area to a positively charged area. Electromagnetism is the term we use for the relationship between electricity and magnetism.

Creating an Electromagnet

When you pass an electric current through wire that is wrapped around a material that can be magnetized, you create a magnetic field. In other words, the material becomes magnetized. It becomes an electromagnet!

Electromagnets attract metal objects with the same force as permanent magnets as long as electric current continues to flow. The current creates and controls the magnetic field. That means an electromagnet is a temporary magnet because when the electric current is stopped, the material is no longer magnetized. Many electromagnets have an iron bar inside a coil of wire since iron is an excellent magnetic material.

How We Use Electromagnets

Because electromagnets are temporary magnets that depend on electric current, they can be turned on and off. The strength and **polarity** of

Michael Faraday

Michael Faraday, a British scientist who lived during the 1800s, is famous for his contributions in the study of electromagnetism. He performed many experiments that proved the connection between electricity and magnetism, and is recognized for the idea of fields of force. Through his experimentation, he discovered how to change magnetic force into electrical force.

electromagnets can also be controlled and changed by the amount and direction of the electric current. These qualities have resulted in many uses for electromagnets.

One well-known use of electromagnets is in junkyards, where there are many objects made of steel. Steel is an alloy that's made mostly of iron, with small amounts of other elements, so steel objects are easily picked up by electromagnets. Since most steel will act as a temporary magnet, the steel objects are magnetized by the electromagnets and in turn attract other objects. Huge, strong electromagnets can pick up objects that weigh several tons!

Enormous electromagnets like the one pictured are used in the manufacturing industry.

Make Your Own Electromagnet

You can make your own electromagnet. Twist two pieces of wire together. Use **insulated** wire to protect yourself from electric shocks. Wrap the wires around a nail about fifteen times and connect the ends of the wires to opposite ends of a **battery**. Place several metal paper clips near the nail. Watch what happens! What do you think will happen if you remove one of the wires from the battery?

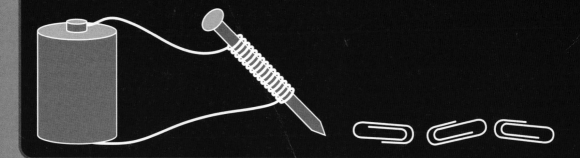

Earth's Magnetic Field

Did you know that Earth is an enormous magnet? Earth has a magnetic field with north and south poles. Earth's magnetic field is so powerful that its force reaches about 36,000 miles (57,900 km) into space. Scientists believe that Earth's magnetic field may be the result of movements deep within its layers.

Earth's Layers

Earth has four layers: the crust, mantle, outer core, and inner core. The crust, or outer layer, is the surface of our planet. It's where we live. The mantle, which is composed of hot, soft rock, lies below the crust. The hot, liquid outer core is below the mantle. The solid inner core lies deeper still. It's Earth's center.

Scientists believe the combination of Earth's spinning on its **axis** and the movement of the liquid iron in Earth's outer core produces a magnetic field. This is called the dynamo effect. The magnetic field forms along Earth's axis between the north and south magnetic poles, so that Earth is like a giant bar magnet.

Geographic and Magnetic Poles

Earth's **geographic** poles are generally what people mean when they speak of the North and South Poles. Earth's magnetic poles are near the geographic

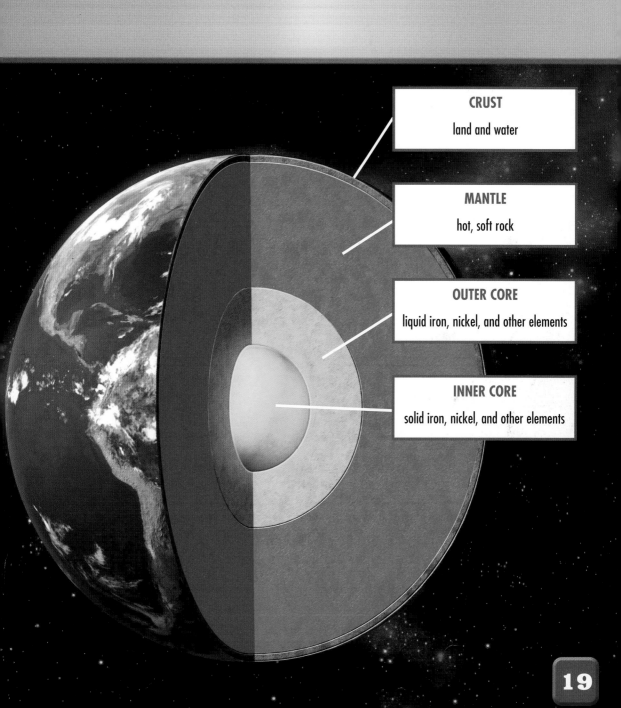

CRUST
land and water

MANTLE
hot, soft rock

OUTER CORE
liquid iron, nickel, and other elements

INNER CORE
solid iron, nickel, and other elements

poles. However, their location is always changing. The location of the magnetic poles changes because conditions in Earth's outer core are always changing. The speed at which the magnetic poles move changes, too. Right now, the magnetic poles move about 25 miles (40 km) each year.

Earth's magnetic poles can even flip! When this happens, the magnetic north pole becomes the magnetic south pole. Scientists can tell that Earth's poles have flipped by studying rocks found on the ocean floor. Scientists don't know for sure how long it takes for the poles to flip. Some think the process takes several thousand to hundreds of thousands of years!

Other Planets

Scientists have learned that Earth isn't the only planet with a magnetic field. Mercury, Jupiter, Saturn, Uranus, and Neptune have magnetic fields, too. Venus doesn't. On Mars, some magnetized matter has been located deep below the surface, which suggests that Mars might have had a magnetic field at one time.

The Magnetosphere

Remember that we said Earth's magnetic field extends about 36,000 miles (57,900 km) into space? That's way beyond Earth's atmosphere. The part of Earth's magnetic field beyond the atmosphere is called the magnetosphere. It protects our planet from the solar wind, which is the stream of charged particles that flows out of the sun. The magnetosphere directs most of the particles away from Earth.

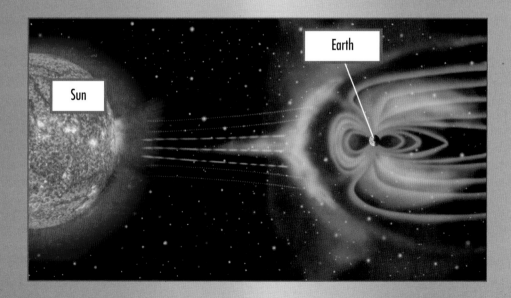

An artist drew this representation of Earth's magnetosphere.

The Auroras

In spite of the magnetosphere, a few charged particles enter Earth's atmosphere. These particles are directed along the lines in Earth's magnetic field and move toward the magnetic poles. Near the poles, particles from the solar wind crash into particles in the atmosphere. This makes the atmospheric particles give off energy in the form of light, which causes beautiful, colorful lights, called auroras, in the sky.

Auroras near the North Pole are known as the aurora borealis, or northern lights. Auroras near the South Pole are called aurora australis, or southern lights. Auroras can be very dramatic! Red and green are the most common colors, but auroras can also be pink, blue, or purple. They look like moving sheets or ribbons of color. Although auroras generally occur near Earth's magnetic poles, they can be seen farther away if solar storms produce a lot of solar wind.

The aurora borealis is a beautiful light show in the northern sky.

Magnets: So Many Uses!

In Chapter One, we looked at some of the common uses of magnets. We read about how magnets are part of our everyday lives. There are many other ways we use magnets. You're probably familiar with some of them. Others might surprise you.

Compasses

Thousands of years ago, people in China invented the compass, using lodestones to help them with direction. A compass works because its magnetic needle lines up with Earth's magnetic field and points to magnetic north and magnetic south. For hundreds of years, a compass was one of the main tools people used when they explored new places.

The magnetic needle on this compass points to Earth's magnetic north pole.

Is It Really the North Pole?

An interesting observation many scientists have made is that our names for Earth's magnetic poles don't make sense. Remember that the pole of a magnet is always attracted to the opposite pole of another magnet. So when the north end of a compass needle points to the magnetic north pole, it's actually being attracted by a south magnetic field! Should the north pole then really be called the south pole? What do you think? Should the names of the poles be changed?

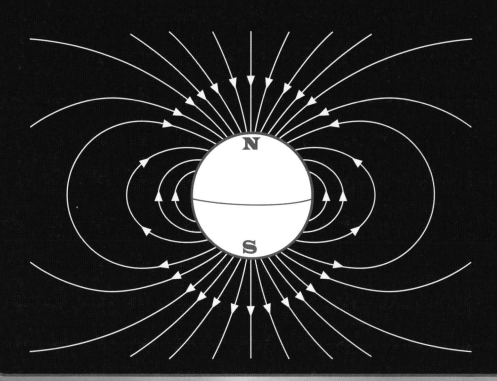

Magnets and Motion

There have been several interesting advances in the use of magnets. One is a form of travel known as **maglev trains**. These trains move through the use of magnetic forces. Magnetic forces elevate the train above the tracks and guide and move it. Maglev trains are very fast, smooth, and quiet. They use less energy to move more people and goods than ships, airplanes, and other forms of transportation.

This maglev train in Japan recorded
a speed of 361 miles (581 km) per hour!

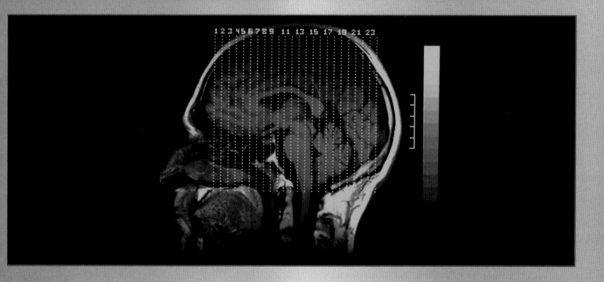

This magnetic resonance imaging (MRI) picture shows the human brain.

Magnets in Medicine

Another modern use of magnets is in medicine. Magnetic instruments are used to remove tiny metal objects from organs such as the eyes. Magnets are also used as a medical tool to identify and treat problems in the body. Magnetic resonance imaging, or MRI, is a method that uses magnetic fields produced by strong electromagnets to take pictures of the inside of the body. While x-rays are often used to take pictures of the inside of a body, images produced by MRI are clearer and more exact.

At first, all MRI machines were tunnel-like tubes like this one. A person was moved through the machine as radio waves passed through a magnetic field around them to create an image of the inside of the body. Today, there are open MRI machines, too.

Magnetic Motors

All electric motors use electromagnets. Electromagnets are in just about everything we use in our homes that has power and moving parts—hair dryers, TVs, doorbells, computers, washing machines, dishwashers, telephones, and music speakers.

Electromagnets are also widely used in industry. In making fine glass objects, they're used to remove metallic elements from liquid glass that would cause flaws in the finished product. Powerful motors and electromagnets drive machinery and pick up tools and nails from construction places.

Powerful electromagnets are used to locate, pick up, move, and place pipes on oil rigs.

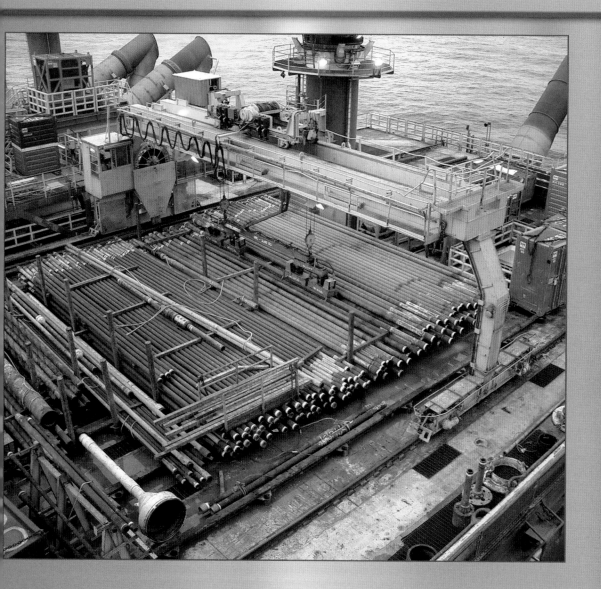

Magnets are marvelous! In this book, you've learned many of their uses. The chart below outlines some that we've read about. How many other ways can you think of that we use magnets?

Ways We Use Magnets

homes	to power large and small appliances
medical practices	to identify and treat problems
industry	to provide energy and move objects
transportation	to provide lift and motion

Glossary

attract (uh-TRAKT) To pull or draw toward something.

axis (AK-suhs) The imaginary line through Earth from the geographic North Pole to the geographic South Pole.

battery (BA-tuh-ree) An electric cell for providing electric current.

electric charge (ih-LEHK-trihk CHARJ) Energy that comes from being positive or negative.

geographic (jee-uh-GRA-fihk) Having to do with a place on Earth.

insulate (IHN-suh-layt) Able to stop electric current from being conducted.

maglev train (MAG-lehv TRAYN) A train that uses magnetic fields to hold it in the air and move it.

magnetic pole (mag-NEH-tihk POHL) One of the places on a magnet where the force of magnetism is strongest.

material (muh-TIHR-ee-uhl) What something is made of.

particle (PAHR-tih-kuhl) A small piece of matter.

permanent (PUHR-muh-nuhnt) Lasting forever.

polarity (poh-LEHR-uh-tee) The condition of having a north pole in a certain place and a south pole opposite it.

repel (rih-PEHL) To push away.

temporary (TEHM-puh-rehr-ee) Lasting for a limited time.

Index